What I Love about Daleks

Nigel King

Calder Valley Poetry

Published 2017 by Calder Valley Poetry
www.caldervalleypoetry.com
caldervalleypoetry@yahoo.com

ISBN 978-1-9997062-0-3

Designed and typeset in Garamond by Bob Horne

Printed by Amadeus Press, Ezra House, West 26 Business Park,
Cleckheaton, West Yorkshire, BD19 4TQ.
www.amadeuspress.co.uk

Contents

For Mary and Marianne

Windfall

It is unlikely that the Lord
would have planted a Bramley –
apples too sour to test Eve,
too homely to hint at forbidden wisdom.

But had the Serpent
a deep Pyrex dish, a hot oven,
how easily he could have tempted
that pair of naked gardeners
with the golden topping, the sharp-sweetness
of a just-baked apple crumble.

So that even Michael, standing purse-lipped,
pointing into wilderness,

even rocky soil, straggling crops
a cold stone hut, scratchy skins to lie beneath,
sagging flesh, paunches, receding grey hair,

even the bickering, the blaming,
wounded silences, sleepless nights,

even fratricide and all that miserable begetting

could not outweigh the ecstasy
of their awakened taste-buds,
the glowing warmth
of pudding in their bellies.

Alarm Clock Heroes

"We'll help the Alarm Clock Heroes keep Britain ticking. There are millions of people in Alarm Clock Britain. People, like Sun readers, who have to get up every morning and work hard to get on in life." (Nick Clegg MP, in The Sun, January 2011)

Six-thirty alarm. I shun
the snooze button's siren call,
heave myself from bed.
Black coffee. Weetabix. Breakfast News.
Pick out a freshly polished suit from the wardrobe.
Check for rust.

Seven-fifteen bus. On the back seat
Gilgamesh, usual thousand-yard stare.
Do Not Disturb.
Beowulf grunts a greeting.
Seems he's had a complaint about his work
from someone's mother.
Poor chap.

Spot Perseus on his driveway
warming up Pegasus.

Out on the ring road
Jason and his boys screech past
in a white van, heading for the docks.
Three Trolls doing Community Service
bash tarmac flat into potholes.
Thor leans on his hammer, bored.

Kalevala Towers: I nod to Anubis at the door,
pat pat pat Cerberus. Hercules ambles past
in orange overalls,
off to clean the Directors' washroom.

How do we do this, day after
thankless day?

Here's Loki,
snapped by paparazzi
stumbling out of Stringfellows,
arm around this week's dryad.
Here's Midas,
welcoming Hello readers
to his shiny shiny new home.

I log on: seven unread messages.
Daphne pops her head around my door:
Morning Mr Siegfried. Your nine o'clock
dragon is waiting in Reception.
I reach for my sword.
Send him up.

Rose

Great Aunt Rose is appalled
by sex - the very thought:
all the sweatiness, the squelchiness.
She tuts at rutting antelope
ruining her tea-time nature show.

A day trip to Eastbourne, 1925.
The girls grin by the charabanc,
in cloche hats.
The boys josh around,
in suits and tight collars.
Rose stands apart, breathtaking,
a smile for no one else.

At eighty-eight, in her garden,
she coaxes tender shoots
from drought-struck earth,
cups a dahlia bloom
for me to admire:
dark red *Auroa's Kiss.*

On the rocks at low tide
I show her, in the deepest pool,
shore crabs and translucent shrimp.
A gelatinous blob of sea anemone
discreetly divides itself.
Great Aunt Rose nods her approval.

Great Aunt Win's Plastic Animals

Her loaded paintbrush strokes
plastic flanks, necks, heads,
obscuring the zebra's stripes,
the leopard's spots.

Metallic enamel pools
in the lion's open mouth,
the roebuck's pricked ears,
the tip of the elephant's trunk.

She pushes back her specs,
holds each creature in turn
inches from her face.
They dry on a tin tray.

With care she lines them
along her white dressing-table,
a gilded menagerie
for her cloudy blue eyes.

At Ellen's Table

This is where we sat
each Boxing Day after tea,
bet on pontoon and Newmarket
with hoarded halfpennies,
her older sisters across from her:
Rose aloof, then riled
by Winnie's cursing at another
Twist … Bust!
Elsie feigning indifference
beating us hollow.

Today she sits alone
at the big table,
takes the bags of buttons
we collect for her to sort,
retrieved from disused needlework boxes,
corners of kitchen drawers,
the backs of sofas.

She lays them out
on the polished oak surface,
matches them in sets:
sew-through and shaft,
plain and fabric-covered,
tiny two-hole pearl,
flat oval black.
She grips her long needle
between forefinger and thumb,
and with strong white cotton
button by button
she begins to thread.

Picture of a Boy

He holds a reed between his palms,
preparing to strip back the green.
He'll run his thumbnail down it
and watch an unbroken strand
of spongy white coil out.

Pale hands, freckles in blotches.
Pale lashes, fine and girlish.
Lips slightly parted, eyes fixed
on the task he is about to start, oblivious
to his father's careful framing,
the focusing lens.

The Giant Takes Tea

Heaves his haunches
into a half-lotus.
The hostess smiles,
black hair tied back with silk.

She pours on hot water,
not a drop spilt, turns the pot
a precise 90 degrees.
Three minutes pass.

She pours the tea
in one flowing motion;
his cup first,
then her two daughters'.

She bows, a precise 30 degrees.
He grips the pale porcelain
fingers like fat tubers,
slops some in his lap.

Her daughters hide giggles
behind their hands.
She silences them
with an inclined eyebrow.

Out of nowhere
    a memory:
in the castle kitchen, slurping tea
    from a tin mug
his wife
    grinding grinding grinding
her pestle
    a broken bough
her mortar
    a hollowed boulder

the baking oven fierce.

A wind chime echoes
in the warm air.
A bold sparrow hops up
after biscuit crumbs.

He nods at his hostess,
her daughters,
gropes for words of thanks.
With slow and painful care

he lifts the cup to his lips.

Excellence

Here's a life packaged
into peer-reviewed outputs
rated for Excellence.
Here's a checklist that calculates
your score as: Disappointing.

In town I buy a tall, skinny latte
with a shot of caramel.
Ashleigh behind the counter
has three stars on her badge.
Her smile is pretty – but is it Excellent?
I fill in a Customer Feedback Sheet.

Excellence flashes her ankles
like an Edwardian hussy,
sets off apace,
a mob of empty-eyed men
in doomed pursuit.

Managers, step away
from your assessment manuals,
delete your algorithms
and look around.

Can you show me
all the Excellence in this room?
Measure its height, width and depth?
Can you weigh it?
Fetch me a handful.

How to Make Beef Pho in Peterborough

Take a small boat on a pitiless ocean.
Add a naval captain and crew,
a good measure of duty,
a sprinkling of courage.

Leave to rest in an army barracks
then marinade in an overspill estate.
Add a pinch of kindness
to counter the bitterness.

Stir lumpy Anglo-Saxon consonants
with a subtle tongue.
Season with years of hard work;
blend, to avoid the mixture splitting.

Bring it together in your own pot, your own kitchen,
in a restaurant with your name above the door.
Serve in generous portions
spiced with the hot chilli of hope.

The Bibliophile

Excuse my presence at your shoulder
and its attendant clichés;
hair prickling on the nape of your neck,
sudden chilling of the air.

They found me amongst my books
at the foot of the rolling ladder,
jacket splayed open, spine snapped.
How he'd have wanted to go.

What sins condemned me
to a century of torment,
haunting these halls,
unable to turn a page?

But today in the café, bitterness fades.
I slake my dust-dry thirst
as I watch your fingertip
conjure words to a shining screen.

What I Love about Daleks

is their emotional honesty.
If it's universal subjugation you're after
at least – like them – do it with glee;
their pepper-pot tops swivel,
their eyestalks waggle
as they ratchet up the octaves
on their four favourite syllables.

What I love about Daleks
is their persistence.
Their plots demolished like Lego houses,
their tin asses kicked
from Skaro to Manhattan,
back they come, tooled-up, re-styled,
yet essentially unchanged.

What I love about Daleks
is their vulnerability.
Their egg-whisk arms
disintegrate foes at five-hundred paces,
their battle-fleets crack open a planet's core,
but creep up behind
you can topple them into a swamp
or jemmy off the lid, exposing to the stars
something soft and utterly helpless.

Glebelands

There's the small field
surrounded by high hedges.
You'll never find your way out
without a Great Aunt
or a dog.

In the big field there's sheep,
huddled down one end
away from us,
that belong to the Sheep Man
whose son fell from a pylon.

There's the ruined piggery
round the back
where Grandad raised a fat sow
in the war, and took himself
to the outside lavvy
when the abattoir lorry came.

There's the empty stable.
Long ago two goats
ate the pictures from *National Geographic*
Winnie pasted to the walls.

There's the Empire of Woodlice
in the hollow beneath
the lightning-struck elm,
a world we played in
for a hundred years
one blazing afternoon.

Yours Is No Disgrace

(i.m. Chris Lees)

Three lads, one girl, squashed
on a student bed. You, filling the only chair.
Spliff smoked down to the roach,
stubbed out in a saucer beside you.

Something defiantly out of fashion
blasts from a C90 cassette.

You lean back, beatific,
as that bass line kicks in,
fingers on automatic,
picking it out in mid-air.

Thirty years vanished.

I sit alone on another narrow bed,
flyers, papers, USB sticks
strewn across a grey blanket.

Music shuffles through my headphones
and there's that bass line;

I follow your ghost-fingers
precise and certain
down invisible frets,
unseen strings.

The Pooker-man

The Pooker-man is coming for our bones.
Quick, fling him the picked-over chicken carcass,
fish that cod's head from the bin.

The dog knows something's up.
She cowers behind the armchair, teeth bared,
snarl strangled into a whimper.

If he tips the peak of his cap
and we catch his gaze
our flesh will in an instant
melt.
          He'll lead us, skeletons, by the hand
to his rattling cart.

Why can't we look away?
We poke our heads around the net curtains,
as he turns towards us.
A raised arm, the swish
of his long coat.

Drop to the floor, hardly dare breathe
until our mother, our exorcist,
clatters the front door chain:
Nothing for you today, thank you!

When we look again, in a minute, maybe two,
he will be gone.

These Are the Hats

This is the hat
I ferried fossils in,
hopping from rock to rock
while my neck and shoulders blistered.

This is the hat,
one of a garish five,
knitted by our half-blind aunt
for the orphans.

This is the hat
I thought I could get away with
strolling down St Dunstan's,
Waterloo Lily under my arm.

This is the hat
fashioned from 1930s' rabbit-fur
my Grandma wore
against the bitter wind.

This is the hat
a sour-faced functionary
barked at me to remove
in Cologne cathedral.

This is the hat
Great Great Uncle Alpine
bartered from a Yukon trader
for a pouch of tobacco.

This is the hat
I posed in for a cartoon portrait
a stone's throw away
from the site of a massacre.

Tell

A layer-cake of civilisations.

Slide the core sample
onto the sterile lab bench,

same red earth runs
the whole way through,

but here's flecks of bone
from the ethnically impure,

here's musket balls
flattened on impact,

here's a slice of flayed skin
from the defeated general,

here's ashes from the citadel
that refused its tribute.

And right at the base
a fragment of the clay breast

of a tiny earth goddess,
smooth and round and filled

with life to come.

Our New House

Once it was another house.
The inhabitants' ways were odd, so we're told.
One night they scrambled what they could
into a cart, and were gone.

For days, weeks, months, years,
neighbours took what they might use,
left a shambles of stone,
rotting joists, broken beams.

In time, someone drew up plans,
cleared the site, raised new walls,
floors, windows, a roof
on the old, deep foundations.

This is our new home.
We have filled it with new things
from online retailers,
out-of-town superstores.
We keep it clean.

We ask our friends around for drinks,
entertain at Christmas,
shoo cats off the patio,
relax on our immaculate sofa.

We do not talk about the night.

We lie in the dark,
ears stopped, eyes screwed shut,
and wait for the new day.

Anima

Unseen at night I try that slinky
slide across the floor,
rubbing against a table leg,
imagine stepping out
to prowl the moonlit orchard
or spring up on the garden gate.

Free the inner feline!
But my purr emerges
a strangled yelp
and my self-willed scrappy tail
crashes an egg-box
to the floor.

Without a thought
I slobber the mess up,
can't help it;
prey to these mongrel appetites,
instead of picking
fussily at titbits.

Owners are oblivious,
just think me *a bit of a character*,
strangely moody, with an ill-considered
fondness for laps
(and hopeless when it comes to
games of throw and fetch).

Other dogs can sense
something's not quite right
(the brighter ones at least).
Last week a Border collie
fixed me with a knowing gaze. I was terrified
he'd out me to a passing Doberman.

I remember a smaller me
slipping under the fence,
to stare through next-door's cat flap.
Inside, a red velvet bed,
a heated cushion, a dish of biscuits
shaped like tiny fish.

The Futility Room

How many times have I found myself here,
bewildered? Is there a clue
in the cluster of silverfish
that scatter like conspirators?

Or in the open mouth of the washing-machine,
one red sock lolling out,
and amidst the tangle of damp clothes
a pair of yellow staring eyes?

Above the freezer's hum
an astronomer on the morning news
is breathless over the first sight
of the ice-plains of Pluto.

Slowly, slowly I retrace
my steps to the kitchen,
glimpse for a moment a golden
filament of connection

between the sink-plunger
I clutch in my left hand
and the jar of pickled beetroot
in my right.

The Perseids

He promised her a stellar anniversary date.
Bastard! she thought,
as she lay on a lumpy sun-lounger

in her little black dress and pearls,
squinting into the late summer night
for the occasional sputter of a meteorite.

We are all comet dust, he pronounced,
rising to return to the house;
but only a few of us can blaze!

No jury will convict, she muttered
as she drove the garden shears
firmly between his shoulders.

The House of Forlorn Ladies

Fitzpatrick's Mobile Library
draws up on Queen Alexandra Avenue.
Win and Cath lug the crate
to the step of number 93.

The usual routine:
first, down to the basement apartment
of the Misses Merryweather.
Damp seeps into pores,
tickles lungs. Win and Cath note
the tidemark round the parlour walls.
The Misses Merryweather flutter,
twitter to each other as they spot
the latest from their favourite Lady Author.

On the ground floor the Widow Trump
greets them with a hard smile.
Her vastness – swathed in an oriental dressing gown,
crowned by a lime green turban –
blocks any glimpse beyond the doorway.
She selects a Murder.

They skip the first floor.
The one time they knocked,
a tiny woman in a beige housecoat
shooed them away.

To the attic flat,
in grander days the servants' quarters.
Miss Kargasz opens the door with a cackle,
her few remaining teeth
jutting out like chalk stacks.
She announces in an accent borrowed from Lugosi:
Vooks! I EAT vooks!

Back in the van, Win and Cath
check her returns for bite marks.

Among the Replicants

I spot the cyborg in a corner seat
as he extrudes a fine steel probe
into his cappuccino.
How can no one else see?

A trainee barista approaches my table.
She turns her head. I hear
the faint whirr of hydraulics.

I leap up, ricochet like a pinball
off tables and chairs
hurtle into the street.
Behind me the machines
twitter and shriek.

On the pavement
camera lenses swivel in eye sockets.
I pull my woolly hat down low.

In the park I find a bench
far away from the androids
mimicking children at play,
the squadron of spy-ducks.

I swat away a butterfly-drone,
notice on the back of my hand
an alignment of freckles
that can only be a bar code.

If I Only Had the Nerve

It lurks in the corner
pretending to sleep
but I know it's ready
to swallow me whole.

I fumble my feet into the paws,
pull up the body.
A boy helps me straighten
the straggly mane.

I step out the door,
into the hubbub on the lot.
Two Munchkins smirk
as I trip on my tail:
Hey Fatso! Hittin' the bottle so early!

After an hour in make-up
I emerge, bright eyes, bold whiskers,
whispering over and over
If I only had the nerve. If I only had the nerve.

I head towards the yellow bricks.

Let's Dance

The lads have claimed their territory
in the corner by the bar.
They jostle, bump fists, neck shots,
try it on with the tall girl and her quiet mate.
From time to time one breaks from the pack,
half-minces, half-struts onto the sprung floor,
every move a smirking parody of fun.

Tom is different. They're playing his song,
the one that was on repeat in his head
when he walked back from Karen's
at four in the morning.
He sways, leaps, flicks hair from his face,
mouths every lyric, eyes tight shut.
At the crash of the last chord
he reaches one ecstatic hand
up towards the glitter ball.

The lads will have little choice
but to kick his head in.

Sending a Man

Tried coaxing, tried cursing,
squirting WD40 in all the joints.
Tried beating it with my fists,
weeping alone in the bathroom.
So they are sending round a man.

He wears dust-grey jeans,
a threadbare sweatshirt
Fruit of the Loom in faded letters.
I give him a hand with his toolbox,
hide a grimace
as my lower back spasms.

How does he take it?
Strong, white, three sugars.
He grunts approval: decent cuppa.
I catch myself almost flushing.
He gets on with it.

Hovering, helpless, I mangle my answers
to technical questions,
pass the wrong implements.
He plays Absolute Radio
on a paint-stained ghetto blaster,
singing along to The Boss:
It's the working, the working, just the working life.

I leave him to it.

Ground Elder

Aegopodium podagraria:
another thing the Romans brought us,
along with dormice and underfloor heating,
masterwort, goutweed, snow-in-the-mountains:
regenerates from the smallest fragment of fibre.

It appeared in a corner behind the pond
ten years after they'd uprooted
from suburban Essex to the Welsh borders.
My father battled it back,
but season on season it crept
through roses, irises, lawn borders,
forced him to a fighting retreat
as it infiltrated the pumpkin patch,
the ranks of soft fruit,
to conquer the orchard.

Today, skin on his gardener's hands
grown thin, bruising like fallen fruit,
he takes a last stand by the purple lupins.
I spot the tip of a familiar green shoot
breaking the surface of the dry soil,
keep it to myself.

Nineveh: South Essex, 1972

I find the Euphrates on the map
trace it east with a finger-tip

as Mum shouts up: *Breakfast*'s *ready*!
October trees sway, copper and bronze,

in a wind rushing through
like the chariots of Ashur.

And the call again: *Bacon's going cold!*
Temples falling. Palaces aflame.

The Reality Trip

I'd daydream in endless hours
of Double Chemistry,
doodle rockets, comets, tentacled monsters
on the back of my Home Economics folder,
whisper the titles: *Lost Worlds*, *The Reality Trip*,
Earth is Room Enough.

Their bursts of airbrushed colour
drew me past greetings cards,
Mills & Boon, to that far corner
of the bookshop on Radford Way,
Sci-Fi & Fantasy neatly hand-written
on a sign at the top of the shelf.

Billericay stretched beyond the door:
a scattering of late commuters
walking briskly to the station,
young mothers with prams,
lads in Corsairs and Cortinas
heading out for the A13.

How could they compete
with angular alien cities
under skies filled with moons, star cruisers
emerging from chromatic gas clouds,
the drifting wreckage
of vast wheels in space?

Where's your head gone? Dad asked
as the dog hurtled down the slope
towards the lake, and I stood
fixed like the pole star
staring up through grey strata
for a first glimpse of the Mother Ship.

Fishing for Wisdom

Six days I fished for Bradán Feasa,
the Wise One,
standing thigh-deep in my waders
casting a subtle fly
onto swift-flowing water.
Then on the seventh day
I felt a tug
as something took the hook,
a mighty pull as he ran
for the snags of the reed bed.

I played him until sunset,
tensing the line, steering, letting it out.
At last he lay exhausted on the surface,
and I reeled him in.
I leant down
to free the barb from his lip.
My heart sank like a lead plumb
as I recognised
not the Salmon of Knowledge
but the Trout of Platitude.

Life's full of surprises, he gulped.
Like I told those other English boys,
you can't always get what you want.
I reached for a stone
that fitted snugly in my fist.
Every cloud has a silver lining,
he said, as I brained him.
And indeed, he tasted delicious,
slow-roasted on an open fire
with fennel and wild garlic.

Pepe II's Last Race

(Egyptian pharaohs were required to run a ritual race after 30 years on the throne, and intermittently thereafter, to prove their divine vitality. King Pepe II reputedly ruled for 94 years.)

Again and again I've run this race,
mirrored my brother God's circuit
of the sky. With every stride
I called the stones of our fortresses
to shatter our foes,
the columns of our temples
to lift up Nut's starry dome,
the Nile to bring its sacred flood.

Midday, this day.
Gold in the heavens, gold at the throat,
wrists, ankles of my newest queen.
Ranked behind her, Priests of Amun,
Captains of my Guard, ambassadors
from Nubia, Dilmun, Punt,
grasping Nomarchs,
a knot of impatient Princes.

They watch this carcass
amble down the first straight,
sagging paunch, hollow chest,
lizard skin hanging loose at the neck.
As I turn each corner, knees clacking,
can they feel Memphis tremble,
Thebes quake?

Tongue shrivelled, scalp cracked
under Ra's disdain,
eyes like dead oases.
Through the haze I glimpse
fields of stunted corn, buffalo corpses
split open like seed pods,
Egyptian blood on Egyptian swords.

The crowd's uncertain cheer
greets my stumble to the line.

Far West

Museum of Anthropology, University of British Columbia

A tall, slender girl
poses for her Chinese friend
amongst the Totems.

Masks face east through glass.
Five nations crowd round our guide.
Seal, bear, wolf all watch.

The first men huddle
inside their clam. Raven thinks:
what have I released?

Heron tops a pole,
still as a carving, then turns
towards the ocean.

Getting On

My Grandma scales the airing cupboard
like the north face of the Eiger;
fingers scrabble for holds on the slats,
feet grope for the copper band
around the lagging.

I can reach the neatly folded sheets
barely lifting my arms,
but she'll have none of it;
I'm fine dear. Go help your Grandad.

The garden is modest, but he's
back in his North Devon acres,
building up the pyre with dry twigs,
cardboard, old Daily Mails.

Neighbours glower from upstairs windows
as he sets a flame to the heart of it,
steps back, straightens his cap,
and watches the world
disappear in smoke.

Tigger Is Watching the Birds

And they are watching her:
wary, skittish, but undeflected,
as if they could tell
even from this distance
she is not the cat she once was,
not the cat who could pluck
a butterfly from the air
or swallow a mouse whole,
nose to tail,
like a kid sucking up spaghetti.

She is content these days just to sit,
lean a little forward
half-raise a paw
when they twitter and trill
for a turn on the plastic perch.
Except for that one time
she rounded the corner of the porch
to find a stocky magpie
distracted by a saucer of scraps
and the hunter spirit surged
through muscle, tendon, bone,
propelled her forward.

And she'd have had it,
save for a final synaptic
pulse of alarm
that brought her screeching to a halt
like the cat in the cartoons
who (to the beat of frantic tom-toms)
realises in mid-air
he has run straight off a cliff.

Sanctuary

We lie awake and listen to the owl
claiming his territory.

I remember another,
tethered to a post
for photographs and petting
at a place called Sanctuary,
how my hand sank
deeper and deeper through feathers
as if reaching into an old pillow.

But our owl
surveys his lawns and borders,
apple trees, raised beds.
He hears the beating hearts
of mice and voles,
the rustle of a weasel
slinking though fallen leaves.

He's a thing of beak and talon
of outspread wings,
who'll never turn to petals
brushing against your skin.

The Undead Trainspotters of Platform 16

Gave up their souls for eternal unlife;
never once regretted the deal.

They huddle at the platform's end,
clutch tartan thermos flasks
of lukewarm blood,

sneer at rattling 1980s' Pacers,
wait half the night
for the sleek white cylinders
of a hazardous waste freight.

Each opens his tiny notebook,
checks it by the red light of his eyes.

When a pissed young thug swaggers up,
thinks he'll have some fun
with the sad old gits,

they smile at one another
careful to conceal
the glint of fang.

Grandad's Toes

He left them behind in Flanders
the winter after Passchendaele,
blackened by frostbite,
seedpods waiting to germinate
in soil fed with blood and bone.

I picture the shoots breaking the crust,
each twisting and turning
in its reach for the sun:

a honeymoon stroll with Elsie
along the front at St. Helier;

Sheila at Paddington, sharing her sandwiches
with a shy young man;

Jan looking down from the Inca terraces
above Machu Picchu;

Little Marianne, sliding through mud
on an Irish campsite
like an ecstatic eel;

these lines of mine.

Exoplanets

Whispers come
from gravitational microlensing,
transit photometry,
variations in radial velocity

and we listen eagerly
as if to mariners' tales
of unknown continents glimpsed
at the edge of the horizon.

We fill in the gaps
like those old cartographers
pushing back the boundaries
of Here Be Monsters:

a pale green giant
swathed in methane plumes,
a featureless grey ball
denser than iron,

a tantalising chance
of clouded blue,
bang in the habitable zone.
We can almost see their faces,

perfected versions of our own,
elliptical eyes
peering down the years
at the world we used to be.